Hacking

A Comprehensive Guide to Computer

Hacking and Cybersecurity

Table of Contents

Introduction

This book contains proven steps and strategies that will help you understand and avoid hacking and cyber-attacks. A few decades ago, people would be surprised if they heard about someone being hacked. But today, hacking is so common that many breaches make the news on a regular basis. Millions of online accounts, computer networks, and private devices are hacked every year, leading to identity theft, data loss, private information leaks, and in many cases, billions in financial loss.

When it comes to getting hacked, no one is completely safe. While efforts are on the rise to keep people protected online, hackers are continually stepping up their game. While avoiding breaches from hackers is difficult, it is not impossible. The first step in evading hackers is knowing how they operate. By understanding what hacking is and how it works, you will be better prepared to evade them and stay safe at all times.

In the following chapters we will discuss the history of hacking, the different types of hacking that occur, and most importantly, how to stay safe and protected online.

At the completion of this book, you will have a solid understanding of computer networks, hacking strategies, and cybersecurity measures that will keep you, and your data, safe.

Thank you for taking the time to read this book and educate yourself on the world of computer hacking and cybersecurity! I hope you find it to be both informative, and helpful.

Chapter 1: What is Hacking?

Hacking is a term that refers to a wide range of activities aimed at compromising a digital device, network, or service. Although hacking may not be malicious or illegal, most times you hear of it, it is usually in respect to illegal activity aimed at getting access to, disrupting, or controlling, digital devices like smartphones, tablets, and computers, or online services like websites, applications, or entire networks.

Hacking is most times motivated by money or an intention to steal or spy information. Some hackers also do it just for the fun of the challenge or to prove a point.

When most people hear the term "hacking," they associate it with the activities of a skilled programmer that gains access to your computer or phone and modifies the software or hardware to be used beyond its original purpose.

While hacking is mostly technical, not all hacking cases are executed with the technical skills that are typically envisioned. In many cases, hackers rely on tricks and psychological manipulations to steal a person's personal data, login credentials, or make them download a malicious attachment that grants them access to your computer. These psychological tactics are sometimes referred to as social engineering (different from social engineering in the social sciences).

There was a time when hacking was nothing but the activities of teenage mischief-makers that were simply seeking to enjoy the thrill. Today, it is a billion-dollar business executed by rogue programmers and complex syndicates that develop and sell hacking tools to less sophisticated hackers. They also mine information for illegal sale or blackmail. These nefarious acts cause businesses and individuals all over the world huge losses.

The word "hacking" is now an overarching umbrella that refers to a range of malicious activities and cyber-attacks on personal computers, public computing, government, private networks, and business databases. It often involves malware and hacking techniques like botnets, ransomware, browser hijacks, rootkits, Denial of Service attacks (DDoS), Trojans, computer worms and viruses, social engineering, and phishing schemes. We will discuss each of these methods and forms of cyberattacks in greater detail in this book's later chapters.

History of Hacking

The existence of hackers can be traced back to over a century ago. For instance, in 1878, just a few years after the invention of the telephone, a group of young boys who ran a switchboard tried to figure out how the phone system worked. Today, we would say this was quite similar to white-hat hacking since they were essentially trying to "hack" the telephone system to figure out how it worked in directing calls to the appropriate places.

However, in its current form and usage, hacking only became popular in the 1970s and 80s. The term's first mainstream usage can be traced back to an article that appeared in the Psychology Today Journal that used the term in its title. The article, titled "The Hacker Papers," discussed the addictive nature of computer-use, which was becoming rampant at the time.

However, the term "hacker" did not originally carry the negative connotations that it is now associated with. In fact, the first generations of hackers are more similar to white hat hackers of today.

The first true computer hackers appeared back in the days of the early mainframe computers, which were giant metallic hunks locked in temperature-controlled cages.

To operate and maintain these giant machines, thousands of dollars were required. Hence, they were only owned by large companies and universities. Because of the huge cost of running them, programmers jostled for time on these systems. So, the early programmer had to figure out "hacks" or shortcuts that would make it possible to get the best results out of these systems to save time and reduce costs. These hacks were carried out to improve and modify the operating system's performance, allowing them to complete more tasks within a shorter period of time.

But as computers evolved and the internet aged, hacking became a word that earned disdain, as some individuals started to take advantage of vulnerabilities in systems to earn questionable gains.

Notable Events in the Computer Hacking Timeline; 3 Decades of Hacking History

- **1971:** John Draper, a computer hobbyist, discovered that he could reproduce the exact frequency of the audio tone needed to open a telephone line using a whistle from his children's toy box. Draper, who was nicknamed "Captain Crunch," used this to make several long-distance calls for free, and earned himself a reputation, as well as some time in jail over the following years.

- **1975:** Steve Wozniak and Steve Jobs (who would later found Apple Computers) began making "blue boxes"- a device based on Draper's discovery that could generate different tones allowing people to hack into phone systems.

- **1983:** One of the earliest mainstream portrayals of hacking in a movie was in War Games, a movie where actor Matthew Broderick starred as a teenage hacker who almost sets off World War III when he hacks into the Pentagon's supercomputer codenamed WOPR. In the same year, one of the biggest cases of computer hacking at the time occurred. In this case, the FBI arrested six teenagers on the allegation that they broke into over 60 computer networks! The group was named "414s" after Milwaukee's city area code where they lived. The boys were later released on probation.

- **1984:** The Comprehensive Crime Control Act is passed. This piece of legislation granted the Secret Service jurisdiction over cases of computer and credit card fraud. The Computer Fraud and Abuse Act and the Electronic Communications Privacy Act were passed a year later, which made breaking into a computer system a crime. Several underground publications that provided hacking information also emerged at this time.

- **1987:** Herbert Zinn (nicknamed "shadow hawk") breaks into the AT&T's computer system using a computer from his bedroom, and almost tapped into the company's central telephone switch system. The first known computer virus was released on the internet in the same year. The virus, which was known as "Brain," was largely harmless. It simply added a short text message that contained the contact information of a computer service company in Pakistan to the infected computer's hard drive.

- **1988:** A self-replicating computer virus was released on the internet by 22-year old Robert Morris. The virus infected 6,000 systems, which was about 1/10th of the computer systems at the time. Morris was sentenced to three years of probation, and later, formed his own company. In response to this virus's threat, the government formed the Computer Emergency Response Team, whose work was to investigate attacks of this nature.

- **1989:** The first major espionage case involving hackers occurred, where hackers from West Germany were arrested and sentenced for hacking into the US government's computer systems.

- **1990:** Four members of the "Legion of Doom," a group of hackers in the United States, were arrested for stealing data from the Bellsouth Emergency Telephone Network, which could have potentially disrupted 911 services. Three of the hackers were found guilty and sentenced to between 14 and 21 months in prison and fined nearly a quarter-million in damages. The same year, the Electronic Frontier Foundation was created to defend the rights of accused computer hackers.

- **1993:** On Martin Luther King Jr. Day, hackers broke into the computer network of AT&T and disrupted their telephone services. Not long after this, the secret service initiated a national crackdown on hackers and arrested members of the group "Master of Deception" as well as other hackers across the US.

- **1994:** Two hackers nicknamed "Kuji" and "Data Stream" hacked into several computer systems, including that of NASA, leading to a massive manhunt and subsequent dramatic arrest of "Data Stream," a 16-year-old boy living in the UK.

- **1995:** Vladimir Levin, a Russian hacker, broke into the computer Network of Citibank and moved funds to various accounts all over the world. He was arrested in Britain and subsequently extradited to the US for trial and conviction. Levin was reported to have stolen an estimated $3 to $10 million, but the exact figure is unknown.

- **1996:** A report from the General Accounting Office revealed that hackers tried to break into the Defense Department systems over 250,000 times the previous year and were successful on 65% of their attempts. In August of the same year, the Department of Justice's website was compromised, and hackers posted obscenities and pictures of swastikas and Adolf Hitler. They also renamed it the "Department of Injustice." The Website of the CIA was also hacked in the same year.

- **1997:** "AOHell," a hacking program that targets the AOL network, was released, and it crippled the network for days with spam messages, disabled chat rooms, and service disruptions.

- **1998:** A hacking group operating under the name "Masters of Downloading" claim to have broken into the Network of the Pentagon and to have stolen a software which gave them control over some military satellites. They then threatened to sell this software to terrorists. The Pentagon denied the software stolen would allow the hackers to gain control over satellites but did admit to a breach of sensitive information. This event was announced as the most organized and systematic attack on the Pentagon to date. The hackers were reported to have viewed and altered the payroll and personal data of several federal agents. Two teenagers in the US, as well as "The Analyzer," an Israeli Teenager, were arrested for the crime.

- **1999:** In March, the popular auction site E-bay was hacked by a hacker named MagicFX. He destroyed the site's front page, altered auction prices, posted fake items, and diverted traffic to other sites. Other websites, including the white house, US Army, and US senate, were attacked by hackers in the same year.

- **2000:** In February 2000, for over 72 hours, dozens of popular websites suffered DDoS attacks, which overloaded their site servers. Websites affected included Amazon, Buy.com, ZDNet, eTrader, and so on. In May of the same year, the "I Love You" virus appeared for the first time on the internet, appearing first in the Philippines, then spreading all over the globe. It caused an estimated $10 billion in damages globally.

Chapter 2: Reasons for Hacking & Types of Hackers

Hackers can have various motivations. But, generally, the factors that motivate people to try to gain illegal access to a computer or network are classified under the following:

1. **Financial Gain:** Hacking is often carried out for direct financial gain. This is one of the main motivating factors behind most of the hacking activities that take place today. This may involve credit card theft or an attempt to defraud a banking system to steal money directly. Some hackers also make money by selling off their victims' details rather than using them directly.

2. **Reputation:** The same way some people paint street graffiti to push their reputation, there is a subculture in the underworld hacker community that motivates hackers to vandalize or attempt to leave their mark on a website or network, simply to gain notoriety.

3. **Corporate Espionage:** This refers to a situation where one company pays hackers to break into another

company's system or database to steal vital information. For example, a company may hire a hacker to learn about a competitor's new products or services before they are made public.

4. **State-Sponsored Hacking:** This is similar to corporate espionage, but in this case, an entire nation can engage in hacking activities targeted at a rival nation to gain access to national intelligence, destabilize infrastructure, or create conflict in the target country. Countries like China, Russia, and the US have previously been accused of acts of state-sponsored hacking like this. Hacking may also be used as a form of a terrorist attack on an organization or country.

5. **Socially Motivated Hacking:** This refers to a category of hackers that want to prove a political point or advance a social cause. This group of hackers refers to themselves as "hacktivists" (hacker-activist), and their activities are targeted acts aimed at garnering public attention to advance a cause. They may do this by taking control of a government website or network, stealing and releasing sensitive information to the public, or disrupting activities on a public network. Some popular hacktivists

groups in recent years include WikiLeaks, Anonymous, and LulzSec.

Types of Hackers

When most people hear of hackers, what comes to mind is scruffy criminals hiding behind a laptop somewhere, trying to break into a system to steal information. While this may be true to an extent, not all hackers are inherently bad. The perceived image of hackers and media portrayal might make them all seem like cybercriminals, but this is not always true.

As you will soon see, there are different types of hackers. A hacker is someone with knowledge of computer software, hardware, or networks, who can bypass or break security measures. What determines the type of hacker is intentions. Hacking in itself is not illegal. It only becomes illegal when the knowledge is being used to access or compromise a system without the owner's permission.

Based on the hacker's intentions, hacking can be categorized as a black hat, white hat, or gray hat.

1. Black Hat Hackers

Black hat hackers are the bad guys. Someone who hacks with malicious intentions and without the owner's permission is a black hat hacker. Black hat hackers also write malware codes that are used to attack people's computer systems.

Black hat hackers are mainly motivated by financial gain, but they can also be motivated by other purposes. Hackers involved in espionage, cyber terrorism, and hacktivists belong to this category as well. Some people just enjoy the thrill of breaking into people's systems and wreaking havoc.

To sum it up, black hat hackers create and spread malware, steal data and personal information, or even seek to destroy data entirely or modify systems illegally. They can be amateur hackers that try to trick people into downloading malware, or more experienced ones that break into networks to steal private information.

2. White Hat Hackers

White hat hackers are also called ethical hackers. These are hackers that use their knowledge and skills for good. Most white hat hackers are employed and paid to work for companies and government agencies as security specialists. Their job is to find security vulnerabilities in systems and networks.

Although white hat hackers do the same things that the black hat guys do, the major difference between the two is that they do so with the permission of the owner of the device or system. This means they operate legally, and they keep their activities legal by using their discoveries to help their employers stay protected. White hat hackers carry our performance and penetration testing for security systems. They may also be employed to carry out vulnerability assessments, among other similar activities.

3. Gray Hat Hackers

Like all things in life, there are some gray areas in hacking too. There are a group of hackers whose activities fall in this gray area. They are not exactly black hat hackers, but they are not exactly pure-intentioned either.

Gray hat hackers usually look for vulnerabilities in systems without the permission of the owner, but they do not exploit these vulnerabilities right away. Instead, they may report to the owner and offer to fix the issue for a small fee. However, if the owner of such a system refuses to pay them, they will most likely post the exploit online or sell it to the highest bidder.

Hackers in this group are not necessarily looking to do something bad. Most of them just want to get a reward for their discoveries. Some of them may not even exploit the vulnerabilities even if the owner refuses to pay them. But whether they do or not, their activity is still considered illegal since they did not seek permission from the system owner.

Chapter 3: What is Malware?

Malware (malicious software) is a term that is used to refer to any form of malicious code or program that can cause harm to a system or computer network. Malware is an intrusive program designed to invade computers and disable the system or cause some form of damage. Malware can affect computers, mobile devices, and tablets.

Malware is typically intrusive and hostile. It can totally or partially take control of a device's operations and interfere with the normal functioning of a system. Malware is typically designed to achieve a malicious purpose (usually to make money off a victim illegally or cause some other form of harm).

Malware doesn't typically cause physical damage to the system. In most cases, the target of a malware attack is the software. It can be used to delete, steal, or encrypt data on a system. It can also be used to hijack the core functions of a computer and alter data or send out information illegally. Some malware can be used to spy on a computer user's activities without the user being aware.

How Do I Get Malware?

While most hacking cases involve some level of technical skills, hackers still need an access point or back door to launch an attack. If you are being attacked with malware, there are two main ways it can be executed. Malware infection may occur either through a malicious email or internet download. Most cases of malware infections require you to be connected to the internet. However, it is also possible for malware to be manually transmitted to your device through an infected drive.

There is an exhaustive list of ways people get infected with malware. Hackers keep on coming up with new ways to get unsuspecting internet users, so the list of ways malware can get into your computer is practically limitless. Popular options today include:

- When you surf through a hacked and infected website

- When you click on game demos online

- Downloading infected music or video

- Installation of a new toolbar

- Setting up software from an untrusted source

- Malicious mail attachments

To sum it up, if you download anything from the web onto your mobile device or computer, you are opening yourself up to a possible malware attack, particularly if you don't have good anti-malware software installed.

Perhaps the most important tool in the arsenal of a hacker is subtlety. Hackers can find a way of hiding malicious code inside legitimate (or seemingly legitimate) mobile applications. This is why it is always recommended that you only download apps directly from an official app store. Most people don't pay attention to the list of permissions that an app seeks when it is being installed on your device.

Most hackers who use malware cannot access your device without your involvement (usually unknowingly). Getting you to play a role is the final piece of the puzzle they need to solve. They simply need you to open an email attachment from an unrecognized sender or click and install an app from an unreliable source. In most cases, the best safeguard against a malware infection is a good anti-malware program.

Types of Malware

Malware is an umbrella term used to refer to a broad category of infectious programs designed for different malicious purposes. In this next section, we will discuss the most common types of malware.

1. Adware

Adware is a software that causes advertising to pop up on your screen. This can occur within a web browser or in the regular home interface of your device.

While adware rarely disrupts or damages your device software, such malware's major purpose is to generate revenue for the hacker by displaying adverts on your screen. Like most malware, the method of infection is usually by disguising the malware as a legitimate app, or by piggybacking on another application that you then install on your device.

How Do I Get Adware?

There are two main ways your device can become infected with adware. The first method is when you download a program that installs the adware automatically without your knowledge. Adware like this is typically hidden in free apps and programs downloaded from untrusted sources.

An adware infection may also occur through sites. This can affect both trustworthy sites and untrusted ones. If the site is infected with adware, clicking a link may deliver what is known as a "drive-by download" of the adware onto your device. Once this is done, the adware gathers information about you and then places ads in your browser or redirects you to malicious sites.

If you notice automatic pop-ups of dubious offers or bogus virus alerts, then your device has probably been infected by adware. You may also notice new browser tabs opening by themselves, or alterations to your devices home page, like finding apps you never installed. These ads will typically invite you to click a link.

Once your device has been infected by adware, it may begin to carry out various unwanted tasks. While some of these are noticeable, a lot of adware is designed to work underground. It may analyze your device locations, your internet search, and then deliver advertisements you are likely to click based on your habits.

Bear in mind that some legitimate applications make use of ads bundled within the program that may also make use of your location and other information to target you. Adware is completely different and is a menace designed to terrorize your device with ads. The ads you will be shown by adware do not come from sites you visit and may show up even when your device is idle. Other possible side effects of adware infection include:

- Ads appear at odd times or in places that they should not be

- Web pages not displaying properly

- Website link redirects

- Slow browser

- New apps, plugins, or extensions that you never installed

- Browser crashes

- Device crashes

Adware is hardly a direct threat to your security, but it can still be a terrible nuisance all the same. An adware author may even sell your data to third parties that may use it to target your device with even more advertisements. Some violent adware may take over your device entirely and make it difficult for you to use your device without ads popping up.

2. Browser Hijacker

A browser hijacker (or simply hijacker) is a type of malware designed to hijack and modify the settings of a person's internet browser without the user's permission. This malware causes damage, such as modifying the homepage of the browser and changing the search settings.

Hijackers also act like adware as they can automatically inject advertisements into a browser or redirect users to malicious websites. Some hijackers may also contain key-loggers. This is a malware designed to record a user's keystrokes, and is a way that hackers gather valuable information based on the keys the user types when entering valuable information such as their account credentials.

Believed to have first been developed by a group of software companies based in Israel to monetize free software, hijackers are typically bundled into free software that is downloadable on third-party sites. When they are downloaded onto your device, the malware is installed as part of the application's payload.

Most hijackers are easy to remove with the use of a good quality antivirus software that scans the affected device and deletes all the files associated with the hijacker.

However, not all hijackers are this easy to remove. Some browser hijackers are designed to make modifications that go beyond the browser they infect, like changing entry registries. This allows them to stay in the system and makes removing them quite difficult. Violent hijackers like this can affect system stability while disrupting user experience when using the browser.

The most effective way to avoid hijacker malware is to keep your software updated at all times. You should also pay close attention to new software installations and permissions and avoid downloading apps from third-party platforms.

3. Ransomware

Ransomware (ransom malware) is a malware designed to hijack your device and prevent you from accessing your files or using your device until a ransom is paid. Ransom malware appeared as early as the late 80s when users of hijacked devices were instructed to make ransom payments through snail mail. Today, ransomware hackers now order victims to make payments through their credit cards or via cryptocurrency.

A ransomware infection can occur in various ways. One of the most common methods used today is through spam emails containing infected attachments or links to infected or malicious websites. Using spam emails to deliver malware to people is a form of social engineering that hides malware in documents that are made to appear legitimate.

Some hackers may also leverage another form of social engineering technique in their attack by posing as government agencies like the FBI to scare their victims into paying the required sum of money before they can have their file or device unlocked.

Hackers may also use another method known as malvertising, to deliver ransom malware. This method leverages online advertising to distribute malware. A person may be redirected to a malicious site or server even without clicking an ad. An infected iframe (or invisible element on the webpage) may be used to execute this. The server then profiles the user's location and other details of the device using an exploit kit and sends a malware that will attack without the user's knowledge or permission.

Types of Ransomware

Ransomware can be classified into three main categories based on how they operate and their severity. These include:

- **Scareware:** This is a rogue code that disguises as your device security software or tech support. The malware sends you a pop-up message that claims your device has been infected with malware, and you need to pay money to get rid of it. If you refuse to make this payment and choose to ignore the pop-up, you will most likely be bombarded with the pop-up continuously.

  However, your files and the rest of your device are relatively safe. Note that legitimate security software does not operate this way. If you don't have software on your device, they cannot be monitoring your device for malware like the pop-up claims, and even if you have security software, you will not be required to pay just to have an infection removed. These are simple ways to detect scareware.

- **Screen Lockers:** As the name implies, a screen locker is a ransomware that locks your device completely. Once infected, your device will be completely frozen out, and a full-size window may appear, usually with the seal of a notable government agency like the department of justice or the FBI. The message may claim that illegal activity has been detected on your computer, which explains why you are frozen out. You may then be required to pay a fine to regain access to your computer.

  This is, of course, is just a lie to get you to part with your money. The FBI will not freeze out your computer based on compliant or illegal activities or ask you to pay a fine to have your device restored.

- **Encrypting Ransomware:** This third type of ransomware is the most difficult to deal with. If your device is infected with encrypting ransomware, it grants the hackers access to your device, and all your files will be encrypted. To get your files decrypted, you will have to pay a ransom. What makes this ransomware dangerous is that once these hackers gain access to your files and encrypt them, there is no security software able to restore them. Hence, if the ransom is not paid, your files will be gone forever.

4. Distributed Denial of Service (DDOS)

A DDOS attack is a type of network attack where hackers force several devices to send network communications to a specific website or server at the same time. Such an attack is intended to overwhelm the website or service with false requests or traffic, and then eventually crash the server.

Imagine a black Friday sale with a mob of shoppers entering a store through a revolving door. Then, imagine that a group of people come along, and they start going around the revolving door without exiting. This will create congestion that will make it difficult for legitimate shoppers to get into the shop, and everything will eventually come to a halt. This is exactly how a DDoS attack works. All the server's available resources are used to attend to these fake requests, and this will distract the network so much that normal users will be unable to establish a connection to the server.

A DDoS is a massive and large-scale form of attack. To make it work, the hackers need an army of zombie devices that will be used to send fake communications to the target server. To achieve this, the first stage of the attack involves enslaving several computers to build the zombie army needed for a subsequent attack. This is done using a DDoS tool. Usually, the infected zombie computers are not harmed in any way. The network of zombie computers is enslaved and placed under the control of a command and control center. The virus lies dormant and awaits commands from the hacker running the system when it is time for the DDoS attack.

Depending on the scale of the attack, millions of computers may be required to work simultaneously to send a large amount of traffic to the server. The purpose of a DDoS attack varies, but in most cases, Hacktivists execute it, wanting to score a political point with the attack. In this case, the target is usually a government website. A DDoS attack may also be motivated by money. It may be used like a Ransomware to hold a website hostage until a ransom payment is made. Some unscrupulous competitors may also employ DDoS hackers to attack the server of a competitor.

How Do Attackers Launch DDoS?

The first and most important part of a DDoS attack is gaining access to the zombie computers used to carry out the attack. The hackers have to figure out a way to get the DDoS tool into the systems they intend to use. The zombie devices can be mobile phones, tablets, Computers, or a company endpoint.

To infect your computer, they might send an email with a malicious attachment or a link to a website that hosts the malware they intend to infect your system with. Sometimes, malware may also be delivered through a message on a social network. Downloading these attachments or clicking the link will trigger the download of a DDoSTool, which ties your system into the attacker's bot. The malware may also be delivered through Drive-by download when you surf on infected websites. In this case, you don't even have to click on any link for the malware to be downloaded and installed.

Once your device has been infected, most DDoSTools don't affect the infected computer. While there might be malware presence indicators on your device, most people do not spot them since their device functions are not affected. For instance, you may notice that your system has slowed down considerably, or you are getting random error messages. The cooling fan on the computer may also rev up mysteriously, even though your system is in idle mode. These signs of an infection occur mainly because the infected device tries to check back periodically with the command and control center.

DDoS attacks commonly target commercial websites like E-commerce stores and company websites. There have been some huge cases of DDoS attacks over the years. The scale of the attack and the size or type of business targeted determines the effect on business. Some DDoS attacks are nothing but a pesky nuisance. But in some cases, an attack can affect the revenue stream of a business, cripple business activities for a long period, and may even cause permanent damage. Some possible effects of a DDoS attack include:

- Data loss

- Disappointed users that may never return to the website

- Loss of revenue

- Productivity is affected

- Business reputation is affected.

Given these possible consequences, companies with websites that get lots of daily visits, like retail websites, have to take a DDoS attack threat seriously.

5. Rootkit

Rootkit is the name given to a type of malware that provides hackers remote access to an infected system without the knowledge or permission of the owner. Hackers can use rootkits for various purposes.

A rootkit can grant stealth capabilities to other types of malware. This makes viruses, key-loggers, and other malware remain undetectable on a system. Rootkits also grant unauthorized backdoor access to malware. They can alter the login access of a system to allow a hacker secret login access by bypassing the system's standard authorization mechanisms, granting admin privileges to the attacker.

The nature of a rootkit attack makes it a dangerous form of malware. Hackers usually install a rootkit on your system through social engineering techniques. Once installed, the rootkit grants the hacker remote access, and this makes it possible to install other malware, steal data, control the computer, or simply observe activities on the computer.

A rootkit attack is a sophisticated one. Most anti-malware software is not equipped to detect a rootkit infection, and many rootkits can mask their intrusions once they are in, making them even harder to detect. Since a rootkit gains total control of a system, they can easily modify your cybersecurity mechanisms to make it even more difficult to detect or remove the infection.

6. Virus

The term virus is used to refer to a category of malware that can self-replicate. A virus is a problematic piece of code that can cause damage to your computer while copying itself in the process. Viruses corrupt computer systems and can destroy data as well. It is common for people to call other forms of malware viruses. But while a virus is a malware, not all malware are viruses.

The term "virus" as it relates to computers was coined in 1949 by John Von Neumann, but it wasn't until the 1980s that the first real-world computer viruses appeared. A virus is typically attached to another program or file on a system and can be very harmful to the point of slowing down a system, destroying data, or logging keystrokes.

Microsoft Windows computers are the most common target of a computer virus, while Macs, on the other hand, tend to enjoy the reputation of being virus-proof. But this does not inherently mean that Macs are safer than PCs. In fact, the major reason why Windows PC suffers more virus attacks is that there are more PCs in the world than Macs. Therefore, hackers that write virus codes target the operating system with a larger number of potential victims.

However, unlike in the past, viruses aren't as much of a threat as they used to be. The fact is, new viruses are not really being created anymore. Instead, cybercriminals are simply focusing on creating more sophisticated threats that will earn them more money. The main reason why viruses are still talked about is that most people confuse viruses with other forms of malware. So, when you hear someone say they got a virus, they are likely referring to some other form of malware.

So how do we differentiate between computer viruses and other forms of malware? A simple solution is to look at biological viruses' characteristics since they operate pretty much the same way. Take the flu; for example, it is transmitted through some form of interaction between an infected person and a healthy person. The same is true for a computer virus as it requires a host program. A computer virus also needs the action of a user to get transmitted from one computer system to another.

An important characteristic of a virus is self-replication. A computer virus can attach bits of its code to other files and programs on your system, and may even replace such infected files completely to replicate itself.

Terms like Trojans, polymorphic code, or ransomware were used to refer to viruses in the early days. A trojan is a computer virus that gains access to your system by pretending to be another program.

A virus can be ransomware, but this is not always the case. Suppose a self-replicating and transmittable code makes it impossible for a user to access or use his/her system until a ransom is paid. In that case, it can be categorized as Ransomware. A famous example is the WannaCry virus spread worldwide in 2017 on thousands of PCS that required users to make Bitcoin payments to the hacker behind it. A rootkit is not a virus, and a worm isn't a virus either.

These days, dealing with a virus infection is relatively easy. Infections can be avoided entirely, and when they occur, viruses can be detected by scans using traditional antivirus software or more sophisticated anti-malware software.

An antivirus is a software designed specifically to stop viruses. It does this through a signature-based detection system that compares computer files against a database of viruses (similar to a criminal database). If the signature matches, the malicious file will then be removed before causing any further damage.

But while this signature-based detection system works, it is not fool-proof. Antivirus software cannot detect what is known as a "zero-day virus." This is a type of virus that is novel and has not been added to the database yet. But as mentioned, these don't often appear these days, so traditional antivirus software will still provide great protection against viruses. A more efficient solution is an anti-malware device with additional bells and whistles like multi-vector protection and other threat detection features that allows it to detect viruses and other malware and remove them.

7. Worm

"Worm" is a term used to describe a category of malware capable of self-replicating and propagating without any need for any human interaction. Most people confuse worms and viruses, although they are entirely different. While both can replicate within a system and can be copied from one computer to another, a worm spreads copies of itself and replicates without any human interaction. It also doesn't need to attach itself to a file or program in your computer to do any damage, unlike a virus that thrives on infecting your system's files and programs.

Worms are mostly transmitted through software vulnerabilities. A worm can be delivered through spam emails, instant messages, or malicious links and websites that automatically install the worm on your computer. A worm will silently attack your computer, and the infection will continue to spread without notice unless you have anti-malware software installed.

While worms don't need to attach themselves to any files to multiply, they can still modify or delete files. Worms can be used to install other malicious programs onto your computer. A worm will continue to make copies of itself and, by so doing, deplete system or server resources. It may take up your hard drive space, consume bandwidth, and overload a shared network. Worms can also be used by hackers as a backdoor to steal user data or gain control and access to system settings.

8. Botnets

A botnet refers to a network of computers infected and placed under the control of a third party using a botnet agent. Botnets are like zombies that may execute various commands on the order of the attacker. Botnets are most commonly used in DDoS attacks, but can also be used for other malicious purposes, including spreading spam emails or click frauds. It is also possible to use a botnet agent to install more malicious programs onto a system, or to steal data from it.

A botnet agent will remain hidden in an infected computer but will maintain contact with a command and control server until it is time for an attack. Communication to the command and control center can occur through implementing a C&C application or through simple HTTP requests.

A botnet agent can get into your computer in various ways. The most common way is through a social engineering trick where you are encouraged to download a file or click a link. A botnet may also be hidden as a part of legitimate software.

Popular examples of botnet agents include Zeus, which steals data from mobile banking apps, Andromeda, which provides a backdoor for the installation of malicious software, Binutu, which uses an infected computer as a proxy service endpoint and Neutrino, which is mainly used for DDoS attacks and to steal data from an infected computer.

Removing a botnet agent from an infected computer is a relatively simple process. However, some types can be difficult to remove depending on the persistence method employed by the author of the code. Generally, the botnet agent will most likely copy a malicious sample of itself into selected locations on the computer and create registry keys that make it possible to run on the system on startup. In such a case, all that is needed to remove the botnet agent are those keys.

Botnet attacks can also be remediated on the server-side. This is a large-scale process that involves taking out the botnet command and control center completely. An authorized party with the resources for such a project usually implements this, such as a government emergency response team.

There are several dangers of a botnet attack. How far such an attack can go depends largely on the author's creativity. This makes it difficult to predict the extent of such a threat, but in most cases, infected computers are used for DDoS attacks or as proxies for cybercrimes, which can lead to legal problems for innocent people.

9. Spyware

Spyware is a type of malware that is used by hackers to gather information about an attack victim. When this malware infects your computer or mobile device, it can gather information about you, your online activities, what you download, and so on. Spyware may also be used to get your username and account passwords, emails, payment information, and other sensitive data.

Spyware is a sneaky malicious code that finds ways to attach itself to your device's operating system. Sometimes, it is bundled into legitimate apps and only requires you to grant permission to the spyware when you agree to such a program's terms and conditions.

No matter how the spyware gets into your device, it follows the same operation method. The spyware is not an intrusive malware like most other malicious programs. It runs quietly in the background and will only monitor your activities and collect information about your computer as you use it. In addition to the stealthy nature of spyware, which makes it difficult to detect, this malware is also difficult to uninstall.

A spyware infection occurs in ways similar to how other forms of malware are distributed. They may exploit security vulnerabilities and backdoors in the device software to gain authorized access to the device. Such spyware takes advantage of software bugs that may occur during the process of manufacturing the device software or even hardware.

Phishing or spoofing is another method used for spyware attacks. This involves getting the user to click on malicious links or downloading files that give up your login credentials or allow the installation of malware on your device. Spoofing is similar to phishing, but in this case, the email or website is disguised as a legitimate individual or organization in order to gain your trust.

Spyware may also be labeled or advertised by spyware authors as a software tool. This can be a hard disc cleaner, internet accelerator, download manager, web browser, or even an antivirus software. Spywares disguised as something else are broadly referred to as Trojans. In some cases, spyware may not come as standalone software but might be bundled into legitimate software downloaded from a malicious source. Once spyware gets into your system this way, it will remain even if you remove the host application.

Mobile spyware is the most popular form of spyware today. They are particularly sneaky and evasive since most mobile devices don't allow users to see programs that are running in the background as easily as they can be seen on a computer. And because most online activities take place on mobile devices these days, spyware can mine a lot of sensitive information from victims. Both Android and iOS devices are vulnerable to spyware attacks, and there are several legitimate apps with lines of harmful code that may be used to spy on unsuspecting users.

10. DNS Spoofing and Poisoning

A Domain Name System Spoofing is a form of cyber-attack that seeks to exploit vulnerabilities in the DNS server to divert traffic from a legitimate server to a fake one. Both DNS spoofing and DNS cache poisoning are deceptive cyber threats that tend to be difficult to deal with it.

To understand how hackers can use this to attack you, you must understand how your device connects to websites when you use the internet. This will require an understanding of what a Domain Name System is and how it works.

Computers communicate with each other with what we call an internet protocol address (IP). This is a unique ID assigned to every server, and computers use this IP address to communicate with each other. On the other hand, the domain name is the text name that humans use to connect to a website, e.g., "www.example.com." The domain name is used to connect you to the actual target, which is the website IP address itself.

A Domain Name System is used to translate a domain name into the correct IP address. This is composed of four server types that form an essential part of the DNS lookup process. When you search for a website from your mobile device or computer, the DNS must resolve the name server, root name server, authoritative name server, and the top-level domain name servers that make up the DNS server.

This is the vital process on which the entire internet is built. Unfortunately, some hackers can use vulnerabilities in the DNS system to carry out malicious redirects to fake websites. As far as DNS threats go, there are two main methods:

- DNS spoofing: in DNS spoofing, a malicious server is made to mimic a legit server destination in order to redirect traffic towards the fake server so that unsuspecting victims end up on a malicious website.

- DNS cache poisoning is a form of DNS spoofing that occurs on the end of the website user. In this case, the victim's system logs the fake IP address in its local memory cache; this way, the IP address of the fake website will always be recalled by the DNS even after the initial spoofing issues have been resolved.

Methods for DNS Spoofing or Cache Poisoning Attacks

DNS spoof attacks can be carried out in various ways. Some of the most common methods include:

- Man-in-the-middle attack: this is a situation where an attacker steps in-between your DNS server and your browser to infect both. A DNS spoofing tool is used to poison both the local device and the DNS server simultaneously and consequently redirect you to a malicious website hosted on the hacker's server.

- DNS server hijacks: in this case, the hacker directly attacks and re-configures the target website server and redirects all requests to a malicious website. Any IP request for the attacked domain will end up on the fake website.

- DNS cache poisoning via spam: for this kind of attack, the code that enables the DNS cache poisoning is sent via spam email. Once the target clicks the infected URL, the computer or mobile device is infected with a DNS cache poisoning, and your computer will now direct your domain name searches to the fake website.

Risks of DNS Poisoning and Spoofing

A DNS spoofing attack presents a variety of risks. Most notable of this is the theft of personal data. Banking websites or online e-commerce stores are common targets of spoofing attacks. In most cases, the intention is to steal credit card details, personal information, and other details from the user.

A DNS spoofing attack may also be used to deliver a malware infection. A spoof attack's destination website could be a site filled with malicious links and downloads that automatically install various malware like key-loggers, spyware, worms, or ransomware on your device.

DNS is a common tool used for censorship. For instance, the Chinese government uses DNS modifications to ensure that browsers view only approved websites within the country; this is one of the most powerful DNS spoofing applications.

Eliminating A DNS cache poison can be difficult. Even if the spoof has been cleared from an infected server, an infected device will always return to the spoofed website, and clean devices connected to the infected server may be compromised again.

How to Prevent DNS Cache Poisoning and Spoofing

Prevention of DNS spoofing and poisoning is usually two-fold. Efforts must be taken by site owners and their DNS service provider to protect the server from infection. On the other hand, users must also take precautions that protect themselves from such attacks.

1. **Website Owners:** The major responsibility of preventing DNS spoofing attacks lies with website owners. They have to install DNS Spoofing detection tools that scan all data on the server and identifies infections. Additional Domain name system security extensions (DNSSEC) may also be used to ensure that your website's DNS lookups are spoof-free. End-to-end-encryption is another method that makes it difficult for

hackers to duplicate a legitimate site's security certificate and prevent man-in-the-middle attacks.

2. **Prevention Tips for Users:** Users should follow these steps to avoid exposure to DNS poisoning attacks.

- Avoid clicking on links you don't recognize

- Scan your device for malware regularly

- Clean out infected cache files by flushing your DNS cache (Network setting reset)

- Use a virtual private network

Chapter 4: Phishing

As far as computer hacking is concerned, phishing is one of the oldest tricks in the book. While people these days are more aware of phishing, this form of scam is still widely used.

The key to any phishing scam is to attempt to gain your trust by sending messages that seem legitimate, and to lead you to divulge information that would have been otherwise kept secret. A simple way to detect phishing is to be equipped with some level of healthy skepticism when you receive any form of text, email, or social media message.

Early Phishing and the Nigerian Prince Scam

In the early days of the internet, there wasn't much use for email. Most people only received one or two emails per day, and junk and spam mail didn't exist. Few businesses used the internet, so people were rarely bombarded with the promotional emails that we now receive daily. But as the internet grew and online activities increased, new dangers like phishing came to the fore.

One of the earliest forms of online email scams is the long-running Nigerian Prince Scam. This type of email would typically come from someone claiming to be a Nigerian Prince, government official, or member of a royal family.

As the story goes in almost every case, the person would need help with transferring a large sum of national wealth inheritance worth millions of dollars out of Nigeria. Such emails are usually marked private, and the recipient is asked to provide a bank account number where the funds can be sent for safekeeping. Of course, there is no juicy inheritance anywhere. At the other end of the keyboard, the person is simply trying to get the victim to hand over personal and sensitive information, which can be used for identity theft and any other malicious purposes.

In its early days, millions of people fell for the Nigerian Prince Scam, and billions of dollars have been lost. But these days, the trick is a well-known one, and people rarely fall for it anymore. The end goal of phishing attacks is mostly financial gain. Threat actors that use this technique now disguise themselves as legitimate organizations with legitimate concerns in an attempt to get victims to provide them with information.

Phishing is an incredibly simple form of cyber-attack, but it is also one of the most dangerous and effective. In its simplest form, phishing can be used to collect personal data like account login credentials, social security numbers, credit card details, or bank account numbers to be used for fraudulent purposes.

These days, phishing attacks are delivered using spoof emails that mimic popular enterprises, organizations like your bank, or government agencies. The email may also appear to have originated from a personal acquaintance.

Types of Phishing Scams

Although a few "Nigerian Prince" emails and similar versions of this are still sent today, most are easy to spot from a mile away. Also, most platforms have evolved technologically, and most of these emails end up in the spam or junk folders. Still, new phishing methods have appeared over the years with advanced tactics to make them more difficult to detect and harder to evade.

One common example of this is known as "fry phishing". This involves more sophisticated methods, where the phishing email is more polished and is designed to evade spam detection systems.

More recently, many fry phishing scams have been able to successfully impersonate big brands and companies and fool several high-profile recipients.

Another common form of phishing attack that many people have fallen for is an email that claims that the person's email account and password have been compromised and requires them to click a link to change it. Clicking the link effectively grants the hackers access to the victim's email address. John Podesta, Hillary Clinton's campaign manager, fell victim to this form of phishing attack. This is just one of the many types of phishing attacks that have become popular today.

Other types include:

• **Spear Phishing**

Unlike regular phishing scams that target many people at once, spear phishing targets one individual in an organization. For such a targeted attack, the hackers will normally scour the internet for specific information about the person to craft a believable email that the person will fall for.

• **Whaling**

Whaling is another form of spear phishing, but the target is the big fishes like top executives and other high-profile targets. In most cases, the target is the CEO or someone within an organization that has access to the company's financial information.

A popular example of a whaling phishing attack is the CFO fraud. In this case, the company accountant may receive an urgent email, supposedly from the company CEO, requesting a wire transfer to a strange account. While the account may seem strange, the email from which the instruction was sent is similar (or even the same as that of the CEO), and the tone and writing style are consistent as well.

- **Smishing and Vishing**

  These are types of phishing scams that occur over mobile devices. Smishing refers to phishing SMS sent to mobile devices while Vishing is a technique conducted with voice calls.

- **Pharming (DNS-Based Phishing)**

  This type of phishing is where the hacker modifies or tampers with the system's host files or domain name to direct requests to a fake site. This way, when users visit a legitimate site, they will be directed to a fake site where they will enter their personal details.

- **Content-Injection Phishing**

  This is another sophisticated form of a phishing attack. In this case, the hackers insert a malicious code directly into a legitimate website, and the users are requested to enter their personal information or login credentials.

Content injection phishing is also known as content spoofing.

- **Man-in-the-Middle Phishing**

In this case, the attacker positions themselves strategically between two parties. This is usually between parties in business with each other or between people and the sites they commonly use. They then extract information as its being entered or sent legitimately between both parties. Man-in-the-middle attacks are difficult to detect since the attacker does not disrupt transactions between both parties.

- **Search Engine Phishing**

This type of attack targets search engines. The phishers will create websites with malicious content but attractive offers. A search engine then indexes these sites. When people stumble upon the search results during their normal internet searches, they are led to believe that such a website is legit, and they click on them, leading them to give up personal information.

How to Detect Phishing Attacks

As you can see, there are many phishing techniques that attackers use to gain access to personal information, redirect transactions, or get money from unsuspecting victims. The stealth and technical nature of most modern phishing attacks makes them difficult to detect. But they are not impossible to detect. Here are some recommendations that might help you avoid this type of attack:

- If the email, text message, or phone call is requesting that you update or fill in your personal information, it is likely to be dubious no matter where it claims to be coming from. Don't respond to a password request unless it was initiated by you, and always call your bank to confirm such communications.

- If the URL that appears on the email is different from the URL that is displayed when you hover over the link, beware. Clicking the link will redirect you to a different site.

- Check the "From" address of any email you receive. Phishers try their best to disguise the address and make it imitate a legitimate address. But if you look close enough, you will spot the difference.

- Inspect any page you are directed to visit before inputting any sensitive information. Is the page's format and design the same as that of the page you are familiar with from the organization? Logos may appear pixelated, and buttons may have a different color. You may also notice weird paragraph breaks or extra spaces.

- If the mail reads sloppy, it is probably not legit. Hackers often use amateur writers, and you may notice grammar errors, awkward sentence structure, and other inconsistencies in writing. Take a closer look at the text to spot errors.

- Check the tone of the message. Phishing emails usually sound urgent or even desperate. They may claim your account will be closed if you don't respond to the request or say that you have been compromised. Don't be rushed into clicking any link, downloading an attachment, or sending private information.

- Don't download attachments from unknown sources. A general rule of thumb is to never download an attachment that you are not expecting. Malware can be hidden within the attachment and can be installed on your device once you click it.

- Inspect the URL of every website you visit, especially when carrying out important transactions. Check to see if the website is secure before you fill out any personal details or login to any website. An insecure website will have the "Http" abbreviation instead of "Https." Even if the website is legitimate, cybercriminals may easily spy the details you submit on an insecure website.

- If you are sent a spoofed mail, simply delete it and empty your trash. You can help by reporting the case to the person or organization that is being impersonated so they can take necessary actions to warn their customers of the attack.

Chapter 5: How Hackers Hack Wi-Fi

While Wi-Fi offers a lot of benefits, including the convenience of an untethered internet connection, connecting to a Wi-Fi network also comes with a lot of potential disadvantages that hackers can easily take advantage of. While some forms of Wi-Fi Hacking require sophisticated tools, Wi-Fi hackers often take advantage of small user mistakes to gain unauthorized access to a network. This may include errors while connecting their devices or in setting up the router.

When most people think about their Wi-Fi getting hacked, they imagine someone breaking into their Wi-Fi connection and using their internet for free. But Wi-Fi hacking can be used for far more sinister purposes. Wi-Fi can be used to access devices on the same network and track these users. It can also compromise passwords, spy data, and reveal personal information about the person's activities.

Hackers can decide whether to go after the network itself, or to target devices that are connected to it. Once in, a Wi-Fi hacker can follow your device around, track your mobile device across various locations, and use it to access other devices in places you connect to. Hacking your Wi-Fi can also be used to obtain information about where you work or the places you have visited, making it both a privacy concern and a security issue.

To cut down on these risks, you must know the tricks that hackers use to target your Wi-Fi network or the devices on it. This way, you will be aware of the habits that put you at risk and will be able to take steps to avoid them, whether you are setting up your local Wi-Fi connection or connecting to public Wi-Fi. These are the common techniques hackers use to hack into Wi-Fi networks:

1. Sniffing

One of the most common ways hackers gain access to a public network to infiltrate devices is through a method known as "sniffing". Sniffing is a method used to hijack packets of data transmitted between a router and a device connected to it.

When these data packets are hijacked, they can be transferred to the hacker's devices and decrypted through a variety of means. Usually, the hacker runs a brute force program on the encrypted data packet to attempt to decipher it.

There is software that makes sniffing and decrypting hijacked data possible. These days, sniffing is relatively easy for hackers to pull off. It is a quick process and decrypting the hijacked data can be quite easy. It can take as little as ten minutes, up to days to complete if the packet is heavily encrypted.

2. Spoofing

You have probably noticed that your laptop or smartphone will automatically connect to a network you connected to in the past. Mobile devices and laptops can be set up in a way that allows them to remember the previous network and establish an automatic connection with them as soon as they are in range.

While this is a great feature that makes it easy for users to connect to the network they often use, it opens an avenue for a hacker to exploit your Wi-Fi device and network. To hack your Wi-Fi by spoofing, the hacker sets up a new network that has a stronger signal using the same SSID (network name) as the legit router. This will cause devices and computers in-range that have connected to the legit router in the past to connect to the newly set-up fake Wi-Fi router. Doing this will make it possible for the hacker to easily monitor all the traffic and devices on the network.

3. Wardriving

Also known as access point mapping, Wardriving is a hacking method that is used to find local networks in an area and exploit them. In this method, the hackers drive around in a car carrying a laptop, an antenna to boost the signal, and a wireless Ethernet card.

Typically, wireless networks broadcast signals within the home or office premises where the router is located, and in the areas surrounding the building. It is possible for devices nearby to pick up these signals and connect to the network. Hackers try to connect to these Wi-Fi networks for malicious purposes.

In the simplest form, Wardriving can be carried out to use free internet. But sometimes there may be more sinister purposes behind it. Wardriving can be used to access company records and other sensitive information about an organization.

4. Encryption Cracking

Routers will encrypt the data that is sent to it, then decrypt it using the decryption key.

Wi-Fi routers use three main security protocols to protect and secure a wireless network. These three networks include a Wired Equivalent Privacy (WEP) protocol, Wi-Fi Protected

Access (WPA), and an advanced Wi-Fi Protected Access II (WPA2).

The WEP and WPA protocols are basic encryption protocols, and threat actors can easily exploit them. WPA2 is a far more secure encryption technology that uses the Advanced Encryption Standard (AES) mechanisms to secure data. But even WPA2 can be cracked by hackers using a wide range of software tools designed for the job.

Wi-Fi hackers can use brute force tools to crack the encryption key of Wi-Fi routers. While this process can take a long time, it still gets the job done in most cases. There is a new Wi-Fi Security protocol known as Wi-Fi Protected Access III (WPA3). This is a lot more secure than WPA2 and will be harder to break into. But it is still in the works and is yet to be adopted fully.

5. Hotspot Hacking

We all love public hotspots, and so do hackers. It is one of the many ways that hackers can easily access the devices of hundreds of unsuspecting users of the public internet network. Hotspot hacking is an efficient way to access user devices, spy on their data, and steal their credentials like their social security numbers, account details, and credit card numbers.

Hackers specifically target public places where thousands of people go to connect their devices to the internet for free every day. This increases their chances of finding the vulnerabilities they are looking for. It is recommended that you avoid connecting to public Wi-Fi in restaurants, train stations, airports, and other public places to avoid getting your device hacked, and your sensitive data stolen.

Basic Wi-Fi Security Precautions

Whether you are setting up a router for your home or business or connecting to a Wi-Fi network, it is important to follow important safety precautions to reduce your risk exposure and protect your device. Hackers can easily take advantage of user errors and vulnerabilities to gain illegal access to your Wi-Fi network and the devices on it. Here are some of the precautions you can take to avoid this:

1. Remove Networks That You Don't Need from Your List of Preferred Networks

Usually, your mobile device or laptop keeps a list of preferred Wi-Fi networks that it trusts and automatically connects to once in range. As explained, this is one way that hackers get access to your system, and it can be difficult to distinguish between genuine networks and the ones set up by hackers. Hackers will create rogue access points with similar names as open Wi-Fi networks, and use them to conduct attacks on devices that connect to them.

Suppose you keep a long list of networks you often connect to. In that case, your device will connect automatically with any open network with a matching name on the list without warning you, and this can allow hackers to monitor your online activities, launch phishing attacks, and learn about your app usage among other things. Always check the preferred network list on your device and remove networks that you don't want your device to automatically connect to. Keep this list to a minimum and remove any open network on this list.

2. Use a VPN to Add a Layer of Encryption to Your Wi-Fi Traffic

One of the limitations of WPA2 is that data sent over the network can be spied if the attacker can decrypt the Wi-Fi password. While this has been fixed with the WPA3 protocol, WPA3 has yet to gain widespread usage. One way you can further protect traffic on your Wi-Fi network is by using a VPN.

A VPN discourages snooping hackers' activities on your network by encrypting DNS requests and protecting information that may make you vulnerable to phishing attacks.

A VPN tool makes it difficult for an attacker to see your online activities or hijack your connections.

3. Disable Auto-Connect Even on Networks You Join Often

As earlier explained, one way you can secure your device is by reducing the number of networks on your Preferred Network List. The problem with doing this is that you will need to manually enter a password each time you intend to connect to a network. This can be very inconvenient, especially for a network you use often.

A simple way to clean your preferred network list but still make it seamless to connect to networks you connect to often is to disable auto-connect. Doing this will save the network username and password, but you will have to manually connect to the network before your device joins it. You will still have to click the name of the network you want to join each time, but you won't have to type in a password since you still have the network listed on your PNL. This will help reduce your phone or computer's risk of connecting to a malicious network without your authorization.

4. Don't Hide Your Network

Normal network access points send out a beacon with all the information that a device needs to connect to it. This beacon contains information such as the supported encryption and network SSID. A hidden network will not send out all of this information, and only devices that already know them will be able to connect.

While most people think keeping their network obscure this way will protect them from hackers, the truth is that hiding your network is counterintuitive. In fact, hiding your network will leave you open to getting hacked as it makes it easier for hackers to track your device.

A hidden network will notify you that a device is trying to connect to you, since the configuration already assumes that the device trying to connect to it is nearby. This means by principle your device is constantly calling out the network ID to make it possible for nearby devices to find it. So even though it is hidden, your device is easy to track. This makes it easy for hackers to find your device and trick it into connecting to a rogue access point.

In fact, it is even possible that your device is not only calling out the network ID but also giving away details like your work address, work ID, and other details for anyone trying to listen in on the transmission.

5. Disable WPS Functionality on Your Wi-Fi Router

For someone trying to attack your network, one thing that can easily give you away is the WPS functionality on your router. Hackers have tools that allow them to scan an area for networks with WPS functionality to set up an attack such as a WPS-Pixie attack. With an exposed WPS, hackers can use these tools to get into your network in just a few seconds.

The impact of WPS pin attacks goes beyond just changing your password. If the hacker gets your WPS setup pin, they can get your router password no matter how unique or long it is. The purpose of the WPS pin setup is to make it possible to recover lost passwords. Compromising this pin means the hacker gets the same level of access as the legitimate user.

Once your WPS setup pin has been compromised, you may have to get a new router because simply changing your password will not kick the hacker out. Therefore, you should disable WPS functionality on your router altogether. Most new routers allow you to turn WPS off, but turning off this functionality does not actually disable WPS in some older units.

6. Avoid Reusing Passwords for Your Wi-Fi

This is one of the most popular online security tips. Reusing passwords across multiple platforms is a terrible practice, and this applies to your Wi-Fi Router as well. One of the flaws of the WPA2 security protocols is that it is relatively easy for a hacker to break into the network, especially if you have a weak password or one that has likely been exposed elsewhere.

To break into your network, a hacker needs to capture a digital handshake between your network and a connecting device and then load it into a tool such as Hashcat. This tries to brute-force access to your account by trying passwords from a massive database of breached passwords until a match is found. This means that if your password is not unique or has been exposed before, the hacker can gain entry to your network in no time.

When setting up a password for your Wi-Fi network, always choose a strong password. For one, you need a password that will be difficult for someone to guess and it must be unique. This means it must not be similar to the passwords you use on your other accounts.

So even a long and difficult-to-guess password that has been used elsewhere isn't really safe, and here's why: Large companies and online and digital platforms get breached all the time with millions of usernames and passwords exposed. Hackers worldwide have common access to all of these breached passwords, and they also know that people tend to use their favorite password across multiple accounts. This makes it easier to simply plug in this database of hacked passwords until a match is found. So, having a long password is not enough. Try to make your password unique.

7. Isolate Clients to Subnet

If you have a public Wi-Fi in your business that is open to customers, you can secure it by restricting guests on the network to their own subnet. This type of subnet restriction ensures that each client can only interact with the router but are not free to scan or connect to the open ports of other devices on the same network.

If the clients on a network are properly isolated, carrying out an ARP or Nmap scan will not reveal any other device asides the router. Also, in addition to keeping the client isolated, you should also ensure that the ports that are hosting configuration pages are not accessible from the guest network as this can leak information to hackers. In many cases, public Wi-Fi networks fail to isolate clients to their subnet properly. This means anyone on the network can seamlessly interact with other devices connected to the system. This is one of the reasons why connecting to a public Wi-Fi can be very dangerous.

8. Change Default Access

To login and gain administrative control of a Wi-Fi router, a user needs to have the correct username and password. For a new router, these credentials are set to a default value. In most cases, the username and password are set as "Admin" and "Password," respectively. Some manufacturers may set a different default password and username, but these can be easily found online.

Interestingly, most people don't change the default access credentials of their Wi-Fi router. Failing to change default access will make it extremely easily for any hacker that wants to break into your router to do so and take over control of your computer or intercept your data.

Changing the default access credentials is one of the basic things you should do when setting up your router for use. Also, ensure that you choose a unique username and password and not something that can be easily guessed. If a hacker gains access to your router, they can upload malicious firmware to your router, steal user information, access other devices on the network, or even use your router as a proxy for illegal activities. There is no limit to what can be done with access to your router, so the first step in safeguarding your router is to choose strong login credentials for it.

Chapter 6: Cybersecurity

Cybersecurity is a term that refers to a branch of technology that deals with processes and practices designed to protect a device, network, program, or database from unauthorized access, attack, or damage.

Also referred to as information technology security, the goal of cybersecurity is to ensure that computers and their networks are protected from unauthorized access. Government agencies, private organizations, financial institutions, and pretty much anyone else that collects and stores confidential information or transmits data across computers and networks has a need for cybersecurity measures.

With the growing sophistication of hackers' tools, there is a need for technology that protects computer systems and networks to match the cyber-attacks. Cybersecurity is a field that is necessary for the protection of individual and business information as well as the protection of personal and national security.

The Importance of Cybersecurity

There are no questions about the importance of cybersecurity for private organizations, corporate bodies, military groups, medical institutions, and any organization that stores a large amount of data. This is particularly important in cases where a significant portion of data stored includes sensitive information like personal information, financial data, intellectual property, and so on whose exposure can have serious negative consequences.

Cybersecurity is the discipline dedicated to protecting information by safeguarding the system and networks used to store and transmit these data. Every year, millions of dollars are lost to various forms of cyberattacks. It is projected that by 2021, the cost of damages caused by cybercrime will exceed $6 trillion. On average, a cyber-attack occurs every 14 seconds. Therefore, multiple layers of protection are needed to safeguard computers, networks, and programs. As the frequency and number of global cyber threats grow, strong security infrastructure is needed to keep up with them.

Aspects of Cyber Security

Cybersecurity is a very broad field that involves a wide range of coordinated efforts across an organization's entire information infrastructure. The following are some key aspects of cybersecurity:

- **Network Security**

  Network security involves protecting a network from intrusion, attacks, or access by unwanted users. It is the practice of securing a computer network from a targeted attack or opportunistic malware that may launch an attack on the system or disrupt normal operations.

- **Application Security**

  Apps and software used on mobile devices and computers are vulnerable points of attack. Application security includes processes such as testing, updating, and the development of infrastructure that protects apps from threats. Successful application security has to begin with the design of the app, and continue throughout the eventual deployment and subsequent management of the app.

- **Endpoint Security**

  One of the most important parts of running any modern business or organization is remote access. This also presents an opportunity for a breach and a major data weak point. Endpoint security involves protecting the process of accessing a network remotely.

• **Data Security**

The cookie in the jar in most hacking attacks is data. Hence, data security is one of the most important aspects of cybersecurity. Data security aims to protect and maintain the integrity and privacy of data on a storage database, and in transit. An important aspect of data security is operational security. This includes processes that guide the handling and protection of data assets. Operational security includes user access and procedures on how data is stored, shared, and used.

• **Identity Management**

In every computer system or network, every user has a unique identity. Hackers commonly gain access to networks by hijacking the identity of someone in the system. Identity management includes processes and protocols that determine how much access each individual gets and how this access is controlled or managed.

- **Database and Infrastructure Security**

  This branch of cybersecurity involves the protection of databases. This includes the network on which they are stored and the physical equipment that is part of the database infrastructure. Similar to this is cloud security. Since most organizations store data and information on the cloud, protecting cloud data is one of the most challenging aspects of modern cybersecurity.

- **Mobile Security**

  Virtually all online activities now take place on mobile devices, which have opened up a new cybersecurity threat that hackers are taking advantage of. Mobile security is focused on securing mobile devices like cellphones and tablets from threats.

- **Disaster Recovery/Business Continuity Planning**

  This cybersecurity branch focuses on how a company handles a data or security breach if it eventually happens. While most of the other aspects of cybersecurity focus on preventing attacks, businesses must still go on if an attack occurs.

- **Disaster Recovery and Business Continuity**

This refers to plans that are aimed toward helping an organization cope with the aftermath of an attack. This includes alternative resources and infrastructure that can be used to ensure continuity of business in the event of an attack, and the plans to return to full operating capacity after the event.

- **End-User Education**

This is the part of cyber-security that focuses on people. It is arguably the most important component of any cybersecurity framework. In almost all cases, human activities open you up to cyber-attacks. This aspect of cybersecurity is focused on educating users of any system or network on good security practices like good password habits, logging in and logging-out, safe browsing ethics, and what to do in an attack to mitigate damage, among other things.

Perhaps the hardest part of cybersecurity is the ever-changing nature of cyber-attacks and security risks. In the past, traditional cybersecurity methods simply involved defending your assets against known threats by setting up a protective perimeter around it. These days, such an approach doesn't work.

Given the ever-evolving nature of cyber threats, cybersecurity now involves a proactive approach that involves predicting threats in advance and taking steps to mitigate them.

Conclusion

Throughout the course of this book, we have looked at the various methods that hackers can use to gain access to your system illegally, and how to avoid them. One thing is clear from the various methods of hacking; most hacking attacks require the participation of someone in the system. In some cases, you simply have to click a malicious link or download an infected attachment to allow malware into your system. In other cases, your system can be hacked when you inadvertently expose yourself through your online activities or when you are using a Wi-Fi Network. This goes to show how important it is to understand the various ways you are vulnerable when you use the internet.

Hacking is not always an illegal activity, but black hat hackers are common, and they always on the prowl. They are looking to spy sensitive data, lock you out of your system, steal your identity, wipe your account, or use your device as a proxy attack engine to take another system out. Despite cybersecurity efforts, hackers keep on finding new ways to break into systems, and millions of dollars are lost every year due to these hackers' illegal activities.

Hopefully, this book has enlightened you on some of the ways hackers can exploit vulnerabilities in the system, devices, and networks you use. Now, it is up to you to take the necessary steps talked about in this book to stay protected online and stay safe from any possible cyberattacks.

Finally, I'd like to thank you for taking the time to read this book and educate yourself on the world of computer hacking and cybersecurity. I hope you have found it to be both interesting and helpful!